A TAPESTRY

OF

DREAMS, GOLDEN MOMENTS, AND FANCIFUL THOUGHTS

BY KEN BEARDSLEE

First published by AuthorHouse 09/08/05

ISBN: 1-4208-6255-3 (sc)

Printed in the United States of America
Bloomington, Indiana

This book is printed on acid-free paper.

authorHOUSE

1663 LIBERTY DRIVE
BLOOMINGTON, INDIANA 47403
(800) 839-8640
www.authorhouse.com

Other books by this author:

Little Field On The Corner

Kid From Connersburg

Partners

Home Is Where You Hang Your Spikes

Rhymes For All Times

Life's Precious Moments In Verse

Making Every Pitch Count

TABLE OF CONTENTS

A POEM TO BE REMEMBERED

It seems to me a poem to be remembered
Is a poem recited, not only in public in
Front of friendly faces,
But one recited to oneself when the verses
Recall an act of happiness, a love of
Someone or something, a reunion of magical
Places.
A poem that instills hope, and inspiration,
A poem that could be a song with a beautiful
Melody,
Bringing forth a deep sigh.
A poem that you seem to hear in a Spring-
Time breeze, and one that can make you laugh
Or cry.
A poem so great in joy and comfort that it
Is passed from hand to hand, from heart to
Heart.
A poem to banish grief.
A poem that is universal, consistent, dependable,
And lasts, from the budding of the Rose, to
The falling of the leaf.
A poem that can regenerate Love, as soothing
As a hug, or a long awaited kiss,
All of this,
All that I've forgotten,
Is a poem to be remembered.

THE CLASSIC LIBRARY

There's Emerson
Stevenson
Tennyson
In there on those shelves,
So please help yourselves.
There's Longfellow
Whittier
Whitman
Poe and Thoreau,
And Sir Walter Scott and his brave
Ivanhoe.
There's Hawthorne
Irving
Lowell and Holmes
Dickens
Kipling
Bryant
Emily Dickinson too,
A regular whose who!
There's Louisa May Alcott and
All of her folks,
Plus, steamboat Mark Twain and
All of his jokes.
There's Jack London
Cooper

O'Henry and Swift
To give you adventure, a nice
Little lift.
There's Hamlin Garland
Wharton
Cather
Riley
Sara Teasdale and Frost
And Gene Stratton Porter's
Sweet Limberlost.

Poetry, novels, some heavy,
Some light,
My Goodness! How all of those
People could write!

So visit your library
In your special town,
After all, my dear readers,
It's the best bargain around.

BY OAK AND BY MAPLE

By Oak and by Maple I travel
Along,
Humming the words of an old Irish
Song,
Upon my bicycle, my product of
Love,
Except when I'm drenched from the
Storm clouds above.
Up a hill I'm now laboring my pace
Mighty slow,
But soon I'll be coasting to flat-
Lands below,
Where I plan to have breakfast and
Rest up my legs,
And fill up my stomach with bacon
And eggs.
At the same time I'm listening to
New England folks,
With their Harbor Town brogue,
And their seafaring jokes.

I'll find the directions to Camden
In Maine,
Which I should reach by nightfall
If I don't find the rain.
Old Camden, now there is a town,
The place I love most,
Of all the nice sea towns that
Sit on the coast.
A bay full of sailboats their sheets
Full of breeze,
And all sorts of shops, just waiting
To please.
So, by Oak and by Maple I'm off with
A rush,
Past orchards and meadows so ripe
And so lush,
Yes, I do miss my friends, but not
The old strife
One needs such a journey, it's
All part of life.

MY LITERARY HERO

LONGFELLOW

Straight from his heart to his pen,
Pure as snow his every word,
Composing his beautiful songs,
The sweetest the world ever heard.

He wrote of the earth's great beauty,
The hopefulness of youth,
Strong thoughts of the human spirit,
And the power in telling the truth.

He read the generous books,
That produced the best in thought,
Remembering their contributions,
The valuable lessons they taught.

Most poets were seldom happy,
Cursed by emotions, a loss, a regret,
But Longfellow was joyous with all
Of his friends,
His family, and others he met.

And the children how they loved him!
He spoke of them in song,
And when he walked up Brattle Street
A number tagged along.

They made for him a special chair
From an aging chestnut tree,
And many a time the children came
To sit upon his knee.

Straight from his heart to his pen
He showed us a pleasant way,
From his first song to his last one
He forecast a sunny day.

AH AUGUST

And there upon a Summer's day
I watched the wind bend forth the
Hay,
Then from afar I heard the bleat
Of sheep where woods and pastures
Meet;
As I walked this August day,
The slightest cloud had stole
Away,
I found an oak and took a seat,
To rest a bit and fool the heat.

Ah August! A cloud had hid the sun
At last,
As butterflies came wandering past,
And as I watched, a darting swallow
Headed for a hazy hollow;
A fawn and mother so content,
Caught my scent, and off they went,
And from a field of soft white clover,
Some bees swung by to look me over.

Two hours or more I rested there,
Without a worry or a care,
In my notebook, on each sheet,
I wrote my verses, bold yet sweet,
Then leaving said my fond goodbyes,
To all of Nature's paradise,
But first I whispered to the grain,
"I'll send the angel of the rain."

FEBRUARY

February, though you bring forth,
Those bitter winds from out
The north,
How nice when twilight steals
The sun,
And all the work is finally done,
To build a roaring dry wood fire,
Hours before we all retire,
Then watch the popcorn kernels
Burst,
And pour the cider to quench our
Thirst.

February, though you show
Us biting cold and drifting
Snow,
You bring us valentines and Love,
And now and then from high above,
You bring the sun for ruddy faces,
To warm our feet and other places.
And then of course, you have a plus,
Just twenty-eight days, you bring to us.

February, you're not so sad,
January's twice as bad,
With you it's just two months
Till Spring,
So bring your winds that chill
And sting,
In sixty days the daffodils
Will bring us golden Springtime
Thrills,
So take the Winter with you, Dear,
We'll look for you again next year.

THE SAILING SHIP

Oh, I think of the day when I stood
On a crest,
Gazing over the shimmering sea,
And there far below, a ship lay at
Rest, sleeping, as snug as could be.
Spreading its sheets on its outstretched
Arms,
Its flags flowing graceful and free;
The sea-wind was whispering her glittering
Charms,
To the ship that was waiting for me.

As I moved down the hill, a breeze came
Her way,
And clearly she swayed near the shore.
Then her ship whistle echoed far over
The bay
Like no sound I'd heard here before.
Oh, my thoughts wander back to that
New England day
When the sun cast her spell on the sea,
And my eyes shall not fail; my heart
Never stray
From the ship that was waiting for me.

 **BABY SNOWBIRD**

Came forth the Winter's dawning
Light,
With little warmth before the night,
And in a certain tallish pine,
The Snowbirds there were doing fine,
Protected from December's storm
They huddled close and all were warm.
I'm sure within a Mother's nest,
A baby Snowbird takes her rest,
Awaiting sunshine in its tree,
A warming breeze, so heavenly.
Then she will open up her eyes,
And look up at the bluest skies,
For soon your wings will move in
Flight,
Above the pines, both day and night,
But for now you stay in bed,
Eat well, sleep late, you sleepy head.
Your Mother knows just what to do,
She loves to fly and you will too.
Even though you're oh so young,
Perhaps you'll have a Songbird's tongue,
So I'll be listening come the Spring,
For all the melodies you sing,
Remember, no one has a pine,
As tall, as thick, as warm as mine,
A pine that wants you for a guest,
And welcomes each and every nest.
I'll check on you my Snowbird friend,
And count the days till Winter's end,
May I, when years have rolled away,
Remember you each Winter's day.

THE LITTLE BROWN HOUSE BY THE SEA

How I'd love to go back to the little brown house
That sits on the bluff by the sea,
Where the cool ocean winds, can whistle a tune,
That brings peace and comfort to me.
What memories I have, of that little brown house,
With bookshelves I hardly could reach,
Where from its front porch, ran a winding stone
Path, that took me right down to the beach.
I remember the times, from a window upstairs,
I noticed at sea a gray form,
A large ship it was, rising up, slipping down,
Fighting its way through a storm.

Oh the nights that I spent, in that little brown
House, with a gale shaking all in its path,
In my warm sailor's bed, blankets over my head,
Holding on from the storm's fiery wrath.
Then the sea clouds would clear, and in sudden
Gleams, the sheen of the sea reappeared,
The waves flattened out, the sea tide rolled back,
And the Atlantic was no longer feared.
The black wharves were crowded, with ships of
All sizes, could be heard an old sailor's
Song,

In the twilight I walked, to the little brown
House, as the sea-birds tagged sweetly along.
Though I've been long away, and no longer own,
The little brown house by the sea,
I would love once again, to walk up that path,
That brings lovely memories to me.
To sit on the bluff, would be quite enough,
Along with the sea and its roar.
To gaze far and wide, to the lighthouse up
North, to the village I came to adore.
It seems I still hear, the fireplace so dear,
The dry driftwood burning away,
So close to my heart, is the little brown house,
Where the sea and the land come to play.

HOW ARE THINGS AT THE HOME PLACE

Often my mind wanders back
To a far distant morn,
The place I was born.
The house in the country perched
High on a hill,
Where a winding stream traveled
Through woods deep and still.
If I returned, could I once again
Capture,
The rapture,
Of such a sweet place,
Where nature created a kind
Gentle face.

Are the sycamores standing
So white in the breeze,
Do the flowers in mid-day
Play host to the bees.
Does the summer's white clover
Spread a blanket like snow,
Does the walkway still border
The roses soft glow.
Do the vines climb the trestles

With bright emerald sheen,
And bring forth the flowers
That contrast the green.

Is there still that strong bridge
That I built for the stream,
Could I find all the paths
Where I walked with my dreams.
Is the barn filled with livestock
Like it used to be,
Is the alfalfa reaching the height
Of my knee.
Is the teapot still hot for a
Friend passing by,
Does the kitchen breathe sweetly
With rolls and a pie.

Great memories, so vivid, of
Angelic joy,
They brought me contentment,
When I was a boy.

HOME IN THE COUNTRY

Dear friends, it has always seemed
To me
That wherever one might roam,
An apartment in a high rise
Can never match a home.

One cannot raise a garden
Or even have a lawn,
Or listen to a rooster crow
As night turns into dawn.

I love to walk around my place
I do it every day,
Spring, Summer, Fall and Winter,
I walk my cares away.

There's livestock in the bank barn
And crops out in the fields,
Each year it seems I'm more amazed
At what the good earth yields.

You cannot put green shutters
On a condo in the city,
Or sit upon a nice old porch
In Autumn, when woods are pretty.

And how about the wildlife that
Visit every year,
The birds with all their music
And the sighting of the deer.

In fact, I feel quite sorry
For roaming folks you see,
A farm house near nice neighbors
Seems the perfect place to be.

THE LAST BEAUTIFUL COLORS

The sunset, as day closes, is the most
Beautiful of all,
And close behind the falling leaves, the
Last bright flame of Fall.
The tree fruit shows its brightest tints
As it releases to the ground,
And the Autumn moon now beams its best
When it is homeward bound.

The purest blue sky noticed, shows
At the ending storm,
And the prettiest Bluebird can be seen
As Winter snow clouds form.
The last colors of the Cosmos are dearest
To my sight,
As is the brilliance of the Rose, before
It says goodnight.

HARVEST MOON

This night as I lay half asleep
Into my half closed eyes,
A creamy light began to peep
From Indiana skies.
It was the moon, a harvest moon,
That spread across my bed,
And lighted up my room as if
My lamp was lit instead.
For quite some time I lay awake
The glow continued creeping,
Till, moving slowly on its way
As I fell back to sleeping.

A SNOWY WALK ON SUNDAY

All the world seemed to be
In perfect harmony

My walk was really not that far,
No sense in getting out the car,
The snowfall seemed to come straight
Down,
Covering all the fields around.
It stuck upon the oaks this day,
And fence-posts all along the way.

The sun through snowflakes tried
To play,
Peeking out from where it lay.
My eyes picked out a small ravine,
A snow filled stream that ran between,
With full-grown pines at rest nearby,
White sheeted ghosts against the sky.

Twas to a neighbor's house I paced
To see a little smiling face,
And place beneath the Christmas tree
A homemade gift to her from me,
For kindness lights a lonely hour,
Transforms it to a blooming flower.

At visit's end, I'm walking back,
The once white sky is nearly black,
The deep snow squeaks beneath my
Feet,
The wind gives forth a colder beat,
Then down the road I see a light,
Whose warmth will cheer this Winter's
Night.

THE LEGEND OF NEBRASKAN CORN

His touch like a magic wand,
Much as an Irish Leprechaun,
The true spirit of corn,
Was born,
Roaming from field to field,
Touching each and every yield,
Tasting all of Summer's pride,
No single stalk was left denied;
Like the dew upon a sleeping flower,
The little spirit cast its power,
And to this day,
I can truthfully say,
All the cornfields of Nebraska
Are blessed in this way.

TULIPS

What a joy for me to grow
Such gems
These Holland Springtime flowers,
That tip their sparkling cups
Erect, to catch the passing
Showers;
Sunbathing, in days of April
Light,
Rejoicing, until twilight turns
To night;
I stand before the circle beds
And softly draw a sigh,
As the stems beneath the petals
Bend, from breezes floating by;
Oh shame the days when stronger
Winds
Will shake the petals free,
And these quilts of flaming
Colors
Will be just a memory,
But this Fall I'll plant five
Hundred bulbs
Soon they'll join all of this,
And stretch themselves on
Tip-toe
For Nature's tender kiss.

HASH HOUSE A GO GO

There's a little place in Hillcrest
Quite different from the rest,
Where the food is nonconformist
And you're treated as a guest.
With service quite fantastic like
You've never seen before,
And there's a stove that shines and
Glistens,
As you enter through the door.

I always come for breakfast, usually
Alone,
A smiling hostess greets me, that
Always sets the tone,
And that Johnny, or that Andy,
Around the place they roam,
Discussing all the sports news
That makes me feel at home.

Then at lunch I have a problem
For every dish looks fine,
How could there be a better place
To visit and to dine.
I've decided on a sandwich, a

Certain favorite of mine,
And then to wet my whistle with
A glass of special wine.

At dinner time my plate stands
Tall
(Rosemary gets the call)
Two meals for me I figure, for
My stomach's much too small.
There's pictures of old tractors
That's the theme here after all,
And some ancient tools for farming
Resting there upon the wall.

I love **HASH HOUSE A GO GO,** it's
Like a sweet old song,
It picks you up and lifts you
Then carries you along.
In all of San Diego, grand city
By the sea, it's the restaurant that soothes
My heart,
It's **HOME SWEET HOME** for me.

Hash House A Go-Go
3628 Fifth Ave
San Diego, CA 92103
(619) 298-4646
www.hashhouseagogo.com

Oh! My Sun

THE LETTER

How my footsteps quicken –
Your letter's on its way,
And there within my mailbox
Is my sunshine for the day.

The excitement of the moment
When I recognize your touch,
That sends to me those loving
Words
And thoughts that mean so much.

At times it's quite impossible
To gather face to face,
So a letter sweet and well composed
Is nice to take its place.

Those words like sweet-breathed
Roses
That I love so well,
The lines so dear and personal
That only lovers tell.

And it always seems to me
That you are swayed to say,
The dearest things; the kindest
Things;
When you are far away.

What joy and happiness rings
Forth
In each and every line,
From the sweetest little heading,
To the ending that you sign.

And then it's carefully laid
Aside
A special place you know,
Where only hands that held it
Can feel its special glow.

Yes, sweeter with each sunlit hour
Your letter grows with me,
And every part blessed with your
Heart,
Beams with your memory.

CYCLONE

Folks, I live way out west,
Where ranching's the best,
And the sun and the snow share
The day.
Cyclone's my horse,
A mustang, of course,
And we're buddies for sure
I can say.
Cyclone and I,
We sorta follow the sky,
Working cattle that's bout
All we know.
We band em, and brand em,
Graze em, and raise em,
Near the mountains in
Hayes, Idaho.

In town it was said,
That old Texas Red,
Could break a Canadian moose.
So he bet his new hat,
A Stetson, at that,
(Against my twenty dollar gold
Piece)
That he could stay on my little
Cayuse.
Now it was well known,
That old Red couldn't be thrown,

So to all Cyclone posed little
Threat,
So he jumped on and straddled,
My worn western saddle,
And was already counting his bet.

Cyclone took a deep sigh,
Took a look with one eye,
Then jumped six feet up
With that rig,
When he dropped from the ceiling,
Old Red's head was reeling,
And his eyeballs were doing a jig.
After three sideway jumps,
Red was taking his lumps,
Before biting the dust far below.
That ended all that,
I just collected my hat,
And rode out of Hayes, Idaho.

ADVICE FOR A YOUTH LEAGUE HITTER

Get a bat that you can handle
Not too heavy, not too light,
One that covers all the plate,
One that feels just right.
As for a strike, be careful what
You pick,
Don't over-swing, just a fluid
Swing,
And with your hands be quick.
Try to hit the pitch in the
Middle of the plate,
(Or even at the front)
It's much better being early,
Than always being late.
Make sure the pitch you swing
At
Is something you can hit,
Remember, bad ball swingers
On the bench will always sit.
Be aggressive, not a waiter,
Base on balls have their place,
But you must be a take charge hitter
When there's boys out there on base.
Hustle when you hit the ball

Wherever it may go,
An error can happen in the field
You never really know.
Work hard at every practice
Be alert in every game,
In baseball funny things take place
No two games are the same.
Play every game to win of course
But have a lot of fun,
It's important that you wear
A smile
As you hit, field, throw and run.

THE COMPLETE GAME

I journeyed to a big league game
The local team was winning,
Then the starting pitcher was removed
Before the seventh inning.
How stupid, I thought to myself,
His work had just begun,
He had only given up four hits
And but a single run.
So the manager and pitching coach,
The brains behind the club,
Brought in a tall lefthander,
A super, bullpen sub.

Well, I was about to eat a hot
Dog
When the hitter struck a blow
That stayed within the city,
Just how I'll never know.
So the manager walked to the mound
And ordered up another,
A guy I knew was all used up
He threw like my dear Mother.
I guess he felt the ones at bat
Could use some exercise,
For he walked three hitters in
A row,
For me no great surprise.

The moral of this story is
Known and widely spoken,
You never try to fix a thing
Unless it's really broken.
Whatever happened to the guy
Who pitched and worked all nine,
Who wore his pride upon his sleeve
And reached the finish line.
What nonsense that they lose
It all,
Leave most of them alone,
I always had my best stuff
When I was heading home.

The bullpen has its rightful
Place,
On that we all agree.
But using those guys every day
Makes little sense to me.
A jam or two is normal for
Guys who start the game,
Each one deserves a fighting
Chance to pitch in every frame.
Let's keep the treasured complete
Game
The way it used to be.
Even stubborn, modern managers,
Can learn from history.

THE BLOCKER

I would have to say, that pound for
Pound,
I've never found,
A blocker quite like Hiram Brown.
Two hundred pounds I'd say he'd
Go,
Muscle and speed from neck to toe.
I'll tell a story, I'll tell it
All,
It happened at the end of Fall,
The last game played for all the chips,
The trophy and the championship.

Three to nothing was the score,
And all we had was one play more,
We all lined up, the signal came,
Forty yards to win the game,
The quarterback gave me the ball,
A halfback run had been the call,
I gave a fake, then ran out wide,
And pushed a tackler off his stride.

Gaining speed I made a bend,
And with a burst went round the end,
Another tackler dove at me,

With luck I finally wiggled free,
A roar went up within the stands,
From hometown shouts and clapping hands,
Twenty yards to nip defeat,
If I could only keep my feet.

And then beside me Hiram ran,
As only such a marvel can,
And as two tacklers measured me,
He cut them down and set me free,
Oh yes, I scored the touchdown,
But back there on the ground,
Lay the greatest blocker pound for
Pound,
The hero, Hiram Brown.

THE BAT BOY

If no one ever wants me when
They choose up sides to play,
And I can't see why they should,
For I'm really not an athlete,
I'm just not very good.

If the other kids make fun of
Me when I can't catch the ball,
And seldom let me pitch
The way they should,
I really shall not care that much,
I'm just not very good.

Yet, how I love my baseball,
The game I mean of course,
How the kids fly round those
Bases,
The high fives, the back slaps,
And the smiles upon their faces.

If no one ever wants me when
They choose up sides to play,
And I can't see why they should,
I'm still happy! Oh so happy!
Being bat boy for the team,
You see, at that I'm mighty good!

THE ROOKIE

He hit the smoke, the ones
That curved,
He hit whatever pitchers
Served,
He hit three hundred and
Fifty one,
In Burlington.

Then from upstairs he got
The call,
But couldn't hit that stuff
At all,
He hit two hundred and twenty
Three
And caught the train to
Kankakee.

But once again he's found
His form,
Relaxed, he's hitting up
A storm,
He's signing autographs
You see,
In Kankakee.

Young Pete, he's walking down
Broadway,
And this is where he wants to stay,
The money's never going to
Be,
In Kankakee.

BATTLEGROUND

Oh what a horse was **BATTLEGROUND**
I still remember days,
When that powerful black stole
The thunder
From the bays and from the greys.

He cut a hole right through the
Wind
With speed, those are the facts,
And set most of his records on the
Rough, tough, half mile tracks.

How many times I've watched him
Trot
An eighth mile off the pace,
Then with a burst at stretch-time
Come on to win the race.

What thrills he always gave me
At the betting tracks around,
With a little wager on his nose
He seldom let me down.

If I close my eyes this moment
And go back some fifty years,
I can hear the race fans roaring
And his name rings in my ears.

For in his final trotting race
Aged, and half-way blind,
He held the lead by one full
Length
The favorite close behind.

Doggedly he led the way
Close at the rail, not wide,
Then with an eye he saw a horse
Come trotting at his side.

Down the stretch the sulkies came
Their wheels inches apart,
The horses nose to nose I'd say
Who had the bravest heart!

BATTLEGROUND! BATTLEGROUND!
His legs refused to tire,
With ears laid back he stretched his
Neck
And touched the finish wire.

As he was walking to his stall
With him I tagged along,
He turned his head and looked at
Me
As if to say So Long.

With memories of **BATTLEGROUND**
My head begins to spin,
My eyes mist up as I recall how
Much he loved to win.

I've since become an owner
But my eye has never found,
A trotter with the soul and
Heart
Of mighty **BATTLEGROUND.**

A YOUNG BOY'S WISHES

I wish that I could
Whistle,
I wish that I could fly.
I wish the fish would bite
My hook
Instead of swimming by.

I wish I liked my
Spinach,
As well as apple pie.
I wish that I could ride
My kite
A mile up in the sky.

I wish that I could wish
Away
The freckles on my face.
I wish I had a pony
And could ride it anyplace.

I'd love to hit a home run
Every single time.
And buy my Mom a special gift
For a nickel or a dime.

I wish I had a girlfriend
As sweet as Sally Brooks.
I wish that I could walk her
Home,
And carry all her books.

I wish that I could understand
The books on Father's shelf.
I wish that every morning
My bed would make itself.

I wish that I could hug
The moon
And all the stars above me,
And everybody cared for
Me,
Like my puppy, **FETCH**, who
Loves me.

MY LOVE COMES TODAY

As each hour draws closer
My heart overflows,
With each passing minute
My happiness grows.

She's coming to see me,
She's been far away,
What joy now awaits me
My Love comes today.

With her comes the sunlight
To chase away fears,
To bring smiles and laughter
And shut off all tears.

I wait at the doorstep
December's now May,
The Winter's now Springtime,
My Love's on her way.

My spirit is rising
My soul is at play;
Spring's voice singeth ever –
My Love comes today.

A BOY'S LOST DOG

Where are you Jack, my precious
One,
I sense a Winter storm.
Have you a barn in which to run
To keep you safe and warm?

My Jack, I miss you pal of mine –
Why did you have to roam,
Just to chase a roving deer
Who strayed too far from home.

Oh Jack, you lack the know how
To be out there alone,
You should be in your dog house
Then out there on your own.

I'm searching all the fields you
Love,
Listening for your bark.
The snow clouds rumble high
Above
It's growing cold and dark.

Suppose you're wet and hungry,
Completely lost your way.
What if an auto hit you
And you're hidden where you lay.

Oh Jack, I'll keep the yard lights
On
To guide you on your way,
And I'll be up to hug you
Before the break of day.

43

TWO ON A SLED

Now there's Josh, he's eleven,
And Jenny, past seven,
Atop the big hill on this day.
To heck with the weather,
They'll sit close together,
And the cold will soon slip away.
On their new "Winter Glider",
With John close beside her,
Jenny's happy her brother's along.
Who's afraid of "Old Humpback",
He needs a new snow-track,
And "Glider's" so sleek and so
Strong.

So with Jenny just fine,
And Josh close behind,
On the "Glider" they shout, "Valley Floor".
With the wind in their faces,
They cover some places,
That no sled has ventured before.
Like a fast moving train,
They speed over terrain,
With their scarves trailing out
From their collars.
Down "Old Humpback" they bound,
Hardly touching the ground,
With yells, two whoops, and two hollers.

At the bottom the kids,
With turns and with skids,
Stop the "Glider" and fall off
With laughter.
"Old Humpback" we love ya,
Like snow clouds above ya,
And we'll talk of our ride
Ever after.

POP'S CHRISTMAS

Santa came the other night
And left me toys galore,
All kinds of games, and plenty
More.
Well, Pop, he always finds them
First,
And sits upon the floor,
Spending hours just playing
With
The things that I asked for!

I try my best to grab a toy
But most I stand about,
And never operate my train
Till Pop has worn it out.
I'm upset as I can be;
Did Santa bring this stuff for
Pop,
Or leave it here for me!

CHRISTMAS PONY

Ive heard from other kids my age,
Im almost 8 years old,
That Santa is the best
At bringen stuff to all of us
No matter the requst.
So Im writen you this letter
Bout whats been botheren me,
For what I want for Christmas
Just don't fit beneath the tree.

I want a little pony
That I can ride and luv.
One that's sorta brown and white
That's what Im thinken of.
So I want to tell ya bout our barn
That's big and wide and tall.
Could you bring my pony with your
Deer
And put him in the stall?

Theres one I've got all redey
With straw and with som hay,
Jus tie my pony up real tight
So he cant get away.
Ive told my dad bout all of this
And he said, **JUS BELEAVE**,
So Im hopen you can find us
When you com Christmas Eve.

WINTER'S WIND

You know, Winter winds don't
Have much fun,
There's nothing much to blow,
Except the bare, forsaken trees
And, now and then, new snow.

These Winter winds are lonely
Things;
I've often seen them play
With someone's nice new hat,
Or one dead leaf, all day.

How sweeter are the winds in
Spring,
How fewer are their plights.
They have the April fields to dry,
And keep afloat the kites.

48

 **MY LOVING MOTHER**

There has never been a single day
Since Mother left and went away,
That I have failed to say her name,
Two hearts we were but yet the same.

The gentle way she soothed my fear
And made the bad dreams disappear,
And sang to me a lullaby
So I would sleep instead of cry.

When I felt bad and lay in bed
No door was shut, no word unsaid,
She cared for me both night and
Day
Until my sickness went away.

In coming years with sweet goodbyes
I saw the sadness in her eyes,
And when I came and we would speak
Her lovely voice was faint and weak.

It was my turn to bathe her brow
To show the love that I feel now,
To ease her every parting fear
And make the bad dreams disappear.

I was the last one at her bed
No tender word was left unsaid,
And when her hand slipped from
My own
No longing I have ever known –
Her loving boy was all alone.

BEAUTY IN VERSE

There is no poem like a beautiful
Poem
With feelings that run on high,
Lines that can make the children
Laugh
And make the grown men cry.

A poem that makes one happy
And ready to meet the day,
A poem that allows us to appreciate
The Roses along the way.

Verses that speak of darkness
Have never appealed to me,
I would much rather write of the
Sunshine
And the good things in life to be

Beauty in all of Nature, the flowers,
The land and the trees,
The Autumn, the Spring, and the
Winter,
The touch of a Summer's breeze.

Let someone else write the verses
Of worry and of lifetime strife,
I'll write of the joys and
Happiness
That brightens up our life.

I'll write of Love and its wonders
The caring and total bliss,
The importance of a needed hug,
The sweetness of a kiss.

For there is no greater power
Than what true Love should be
It's the measure of peace and
Contentment
For all of eternity.

HOUSEHOLD BLUES

Put all that inside work aside
That cause you so much trouble,
Grab your coat and take a walk
Let Nature burst your bubble.

Just feel the sweetness of the
Breeze
The colors bright yet mellow,
The meadows and the hillsides wait
For such a home-spent fellow.

Take rest from all that stuffy air
Just leave it all behind, if your glass is filled with tasteless
Punch
Instead of sparkling wine.

Shed that pale and sunless look
Those cheeks need to be red,
Lay aside that checkbook
And fish a stream instead.

Forget those old homebodies
Who speak of thorns and briers
There's roses, and birds, and
Butterflies
To meet your hearts desires.

So dig out that old felted hat
That worn out pair of shoes,
Whistle with that Bluebird
And forget those household blues.

I WISH I COULD BE

I wish I could be every breeze in the
Grasses,
Along each path that she passes,
And be each little bird that sings her
Delight
With a tune that is happy and light.

I'd like to be flowers on her window-
Sill,
And her first of the Spring Daffodil.
I'd love to be Roses of her favorite
Bloom,
And the moonbeams that creep in
Her room.

How I envy all things that see her
Each day,
And to each I have only to say,
I would give all possessions, change
All of my ways,
To be with her each of my days.

I'LL NEVER BE FORGETTING

When you're not well, as you
Are now,
I worry so about you,
For when you're hurting like today,
My heart is hurting too.
And how I miss not seeing you in
Beams of day's sunlight,
In the turning into twilight
Before the lonely night.

I wish that I could visit you to
Make two cups of tea,
To sit with you, and read to you,
As you would do for me.
To reminisce of days before when
We would take our walks,
Then rest upon a path-side bench
For smiles and lovely talks.

It's so difficult to be apart,
To be so far away,
To struggle through the waiting
Hours,
To pass away the day.
If I could hold your hand in mine,

Place my other on your brow,
My world would be quite sweet enough,
I'd be so happy now.

So rest My Dear, take care My
Dear,
You shall be feeling better,
Please note my cares, my longing
Thoughts,
I've placed within this letter.
That you are there, and I am here,
I'll always be regretting,
But all your Love, and what it
Means,
I'll never be forgetting.

FOREVER WITH ME

This morn I walked a misty path
And roamed the woodlots through;
How danced your form before my eyes
Upon the silver dew.

In afternoon I was in town
How close you seemed to be;
All those people passing by
No face but yours I see.

At evening time when day is done
Two books seem both the same;
In passages; on every page,
In both I read your name.

A MAIDEN'S
MYSTERY of the MISTLETOE

I fell asleep, really I did
Beneath the mistletoe,
And I had thought that all the
Guests
Had left when lights were low.

But there within the silence,
I thought I saw someone,
And then within a blink of an eye,
The tender act was done.

Not a footstep did I hear,
No breath upon my cheek,
No shadow on the parlor wall,
No voice did I hear speak.

Do you think that I was
Dreaming?
Was all this make believe?
Was it a longing in my heart,
That kiss that I received?

Oh no, for me he was my lover,
The one I've waited for,
And some lonely Winter's
Afternoon,
He'll knock upon my door.

THE SLEIGH RIDE

How cold this Winter night!
All bundled up I step outside,
The snowdrifts lie, so deep, so wide.
The moonlight makes them silver white.
I hear the friendly voices ring,
Clear I hear the song they sing.
Inside the sleigh the quilts are spread,
Who knows this night what lies ahead.

And now we ride three hours hence,
The snow halfway on every fence,
The sleigh-bells ring in homeward
Flight,
The horses' backs with frost are white.
I walk my Sweetheart to her door,
A kiss and hug while riders wait,
Impatient just beyond the gate,
And then our sleigh is off once more.

EARLY SPRING

I lay upon a nearby hill
Of April's newborn grass,
And watched the clouds of early
Spring
Change forms as they rolled past.

In time I rose and walked to town
With calm and happy mind,
And found a maiden's garden
With flowers of every kind.

The fairest and the sweetest
Of all within the beds,
Were the golden yellow Daffodils
With bending little heads.

I stood leaning on the gray stone
Wall
The fragrance touched my face,
And my soul was soothed and mellowed
By the beauty of the place.

The April sun was setting
Slowly dropping out of sight,
With reluctance,
I made my way once more back
Home,
Before the shades of night.

MAY I BE PLACED WITHIN YOUR HEART

When you sit by woodlot stream,
When you walk by moonlight's beam,
When you're alone within a dream,
May I be placed within your heart.

In every precious Nature-scene,
The gold, the red, the blue, the green,
And all the beauty placed between,
May I be placed within your heart.

When you are down and feeling bad,
When clouded days have made you sad,
When cheerfulness cannot be had,
May I be placed within your heart.

When I'm not there to hold you tight,
When darkness drives away the light,
When Love could make it all seem right,
May I be placed within your heart.

I love LOVE

True Love is so precious.
I love Love.
Though without devotion and
Dedication, it can disappear
As morning mist before the
Dawning sun.
All true Love uplifts spirit,
And its soft tones, music, and
Feelings are simply only one.
All true Love is beauty.
I love Love,
For peace; for contentment; for
Completeness.
It is the rain awakening flowers;
The moonlight, and the sunlight,
All in one caress.

THE COMING OF SPRING

The children were starting to shed caps
And coats,
From the birds I heard one hundred beautiful
Notes;
For Nature's big clock had reached the fine
Hour
Of waking up buds, and each Springtime
Flower.

The trees were starting to show all their
Pleasure,
And although I couldn't measure
What they thought of the sight,
I thought I heard whispers of childish
Delight.

On this day I could feel my heart and soul
Tingle,
As the soft rain caressed every roof, every
Shingle,
And seeped into each of the red foxes dens,
As well as the nests of the miniature wrens.

There's the Crocus, so pretty, so early, so
Proud,
As fair, yet as flitting, as any Spring
Cloud;
Like Lilacs, their visit ends abruptly, too
Soon,
Why can't both stay around till the last days
Of June.

Let's accept what we have, enjoy it I say,
Summer's in waiting for its yearly stay;
Then Autumn drifts in with its rose-tinted
Skies,
And so many more colors that dazzle our eyes.

As Winter, and Nature casts its armor forth
With Canadian cold dropping down from the
North;
Yet rejoice, for there's days when the snow
Seems to hang as a curtain,
Pure white, pillow soft, of that I am
Certain.

TOM & BOB

On a nice piece of ground,
Nine miles from town,
Stood the farmhouse of Isaac
McCloy,
Where he had resided for years,
On two little places,
Since a barefooted, hard working,
Boy.

Now most of his days,
He was set in his ways,
And no tractors were used on
His places,
He drove a large team of Percheron
Horses
Stone greys with some white on their
Faces.

Tom and Bob were their names,
Isaac braided their manes,
And showed them each year at the
Fair.
They won all the ribbons, for
Show and for pulling,
A nice looking, fine working,
Pair.

Yet the neighbors poked fun,
When their plowing was done,
For Isaac was so far behind,
But his ears never heard them,
His eyes never saw them,
He just simply paid them no mind.

Then after a spell,
The Winter snow fell,
With winds that spoke fear with
Their roars.
Three days it raged on with nary
A break,
Till the drifts were as high as
The doors.

Then a call was received,
Over which Isaac grieved,
Seems a neighbor was sick where
She lay,
Little Maggie Johanson, needed some
Help,
But the doctor was nine miles away.

What a stroke of bad luck,
For no tractor or truck,
Could drive through those drifts
On this night,
But with a light cutter pulled
By Tom and Bob
Could they make it! Who knows,
They just might.

The barn seemed a mile,
But after a while,
He was there where his two
Friends were bedded,

He fed them their grain, then
Harnessed them up,
Soon with cutter to town they
Were headed.

Reaching the road,
With their light-weighted load,
Tom and Bob were up to their tests,
With precision they pulled, as if
At the fair,
With snow to their bellies and chests.

The wind was so raw,
And then Isaac saw,
Some lights in the distance from
Town,
"Come on Tom and Bob," Isaac did
Shout,
"We're not going to let Maggie down."

With the doctor aboard,
Off the Percherons roared,
Their breath steaming forth in
The air,
Were there ever two horses hooked
Up as a team
That could challenge this magnificent
Pair!

When we reached Maggie's place,
The surprise look on her face,
Let us know we had nothing to fear.
She gave a faint smile, took hold
Of my hand,
And brushed away one little tear.

Never again was a farmer's laugh
To ever come his way,
For plowing five acres with Tom
And Bob
From the start to the end of the day.
Instead in the field they met their
Neighbor,
And the heroes that stood nearby,
Shaking the hand of the Percheron
Man,
With the forgiving look in his eye.

SANTA FE RANCH

Today, my thoughts of the old ranch
Are fresh on my mind,
So many sweet memories that I left
Behind;
The southwestern cowboys so kind and
So dear,
Their campfire songs that I so loved
To hear.

There's so much to say, just where
Should I start,
For each memory lies ever close to
My heart;
The ranch, the land, the cattle and
Such,
Hard riding Curley, I miss him so much.

Standing here now, what waste and
Decay,
How all of the beauty has now passed
Away;
On the bunkhouse there hangs an old
Broken door,
And inside there's sagebrush all
Over the floor.

There's an old Empire stove all
Covered with dust,
And a busted down rifle its bore
Filled with rust;
There's a couple old horseshoes nailed
To the wall,
And the whole place is leaning,
About ready to fall.

I still remember, there was always
A meal for a drifting cowpoke,
And a days work just waiting when
Mustangs were broke;
And the laughter, the smiles all
Around,
When the hands took their new hats
And headed to town.

Kindhearted Curley, who pulled
Me aside,
And on his own time, taught me to
Ride;
He taught me to rope, how to play
The guitar,
How to travel at night by just
Watching a star.

How beautiful the sun sets far
Off in the west,
Mother Nature wears sainthood when
Showing her best;
A fine brush-stroked painting with
Soft purple glow,
It soothes me, yet tells me, it's
Now time to go.

I've lost track of Curley, with
His spirit and flair,
But I'm sure he's still singing,
And riding somewhere;
I'll be back again next year, you
Couldn't keep me away,
From the ranch of my boyhood,
Near Old Santa Fe.

HIBERNATION

Are the trees really crying –
The late flowers sighing –
To see the year dying,
But I can truthfully say I simply
Retire,
And while the cold north wind sings,
I just accept what it brings,
Read my favorite things
Before a nice roaring fire.

I feel I'm really self-taught –
With the books that I've bought –
Isn't that a nice thought
To have on this wild Winter's night!
So let the snow drift hip deep –
Charming hours I will keep –
Before nodding and falling to sleep
Until waking to dawn's early light.

ONE AND ANOTHER

George Conklin I know is a
Peach of a fellow,
With a warm disposition, sort
Of quiet and mellow.

Treats everyone like a dear
Loving brother,
He's kind to his dog, and he's
Sweet to his mother.

Never chews that tobacco in
Games you might know,
And the kids think he's **BABE,**
Cause he pleases them so.

He maintains a smile when he's
Caught in a slump,
Never raises his voice to a
Near-sighted ump.

But I'm here in this verse
For the guy makes me sick,
Although he's a sweetheart,
He can't hit a lick.